Join the Action

Six Plays to Read or Record

Paul Groves
Head of the English Department
St Hugh's C.E. Secondary Modern School Grantham

Nigel Grimshaw
Senior Lecturer in English
Kesteven College of Education Stoke Rochford

Edward Arnold

© Paul Groves and Nigel Grimshaw 1973

First published 1973
by Edward Arnold (Publishers) Ltd.,
25 Hill Street,
London W1X 8LL

Reprinted 1974, 1975, 1976.

ISBN: 0 7131 1820 2

Printed in Great Britain by
Unwin Brothers Limited, Old Woking, Surrey

Contents

These plays are for reading in groups, for tape recording or performance in the classroom. All of them contain eight or more characters.

Dave and the Dog

Characters:

Martin *Barry*
Dave *Ross*
Anne-Marie *Julie*
Mum *Amanda*
Dad *Paul*
Fiona *Kimberley*
A Policeman *Robert*
A Burglar *Graeme*

Waste ground near a river.

Martin	'Ello, Dave. How are you doing?
Dave	O.K. Are you coming down town?
Martin	No, I've got my dog.
Dave	Where is he?
Martin	Over there, behind those bushes. I think he's got a rat or something.
Dave	Let's go and see.
	(*Sound of a dog digging*)
Martin	Go it, boy!
Dave	Just look at that dirt flying. He's better than a mechanical digger.
Martin	Go it, boy.
Dave	There's nothing there.

Martin	You've had it this time, boy.
Dave	I wish I had a dog.
Martin	I can get you one.
Dave	No, it's my old man. He won't let me have one in the house.
Martin	Hard luck.
Dave	Just wait till I have a house of my own. I'll fill it with dogs. I'll have boxers and sheep dogs and Dalmatians all over the place.
Martin	They'll fight like mad.
Dave	No, I'll train them.
Martin	Here comes that stuck-up Anne-Marie with her poodle.

(*Sound of barks*)

Anne-Marie	Get your dog off, Martin.
Martin	He's all right. He's only playing.
Anne-Marie	Get him off. He'll bite Betsy.
Martin	He won't. I think he fancies her.
Anne-Marie	Get him off. He's a rough dog.
Martin	Come here, boy. Come here. Now sit. Sit, I say. There you are, see. What an obedient dog he is and what a brilliant trainer I am. Rough, you say?
Anne-Marie	I think you should keep him on a lead.
Martin	Don't believe in it. Dogs should be free. Like people.
Anne-Marie	Come on, Betsy.
Martin	You see, she won't go away. They like each other.
Anne-Marie	You naughty dog.

(*The boys laugh*)

Martin	Trust her to have a dog like that. She's afraid to get it dirty. What a cissie dog to have.
Dave	You know what, Mart? If my Dad would let me have a poodle, I'd have one like a shot.
Martin	Garn, not a poodle.
Dave	Yeh.

8

Martin	You must need one badly.
Dave	Yeh, and whatever dog I have I'm going to call it Tiger.
Martin	Funny name for a dog.
Dave	I read it in a book once.

(*Fade*)

Dave's house.

Mum	Make sure you wash your hands before having dinner, David.
Dave	O.K.
Mum	Have you seen Fiona?
Dave	No.
Mum	Just like her to be missing at mealtimes. Where have you been?
Dave	In the park. Cor, you should have seen Martin's dog. It was after a rat. You should see it dig. Like a mechanical digger.
Mum	I know what you're hinting at.
Dave	Don't you think we could have one, Mum?
Mum	I'd like one for company, especially when you're all out like this morning. But it's up to your father and you know what he thinks.
Dave	Silly fool.
Mum	David! Don't speak like that about your father. Here he is.
Dad	Hello, Mum. What's for dinner?
Mum	Steak and kidney pie.
Dad	I'll just change.
Mum	I should think so. He looks in a good mood. Go and try once more.

(*Fade*)

Dad	(*Whistling*) Hello, David. I can't wait to get my teeth in that steak and kidney. I bet you're hungry. Or you ought to be.

Dave	Dad, can I have a dog?
Dad	Now look, I thought I'd made it plain. No dogs.
Dave	But, Dad.
Dad	Under no circumstances am I having a dog in this house.
Dave	Why?
Dad	You know very well why: they smell; they cost more than we can afford; and there's all that trouble when you go away.
Dave	But Dad—
Dad	No, and that's final.
Mum	Couldn't we, Ernest?
Dad	Don't you start.
Mum	Where are you going, David?
Dave	Out.
Mum	But your dinner—
Dad	Come back here, lad. Come back.

(*Door slams*)

Mum	You've really upset him. Now his dinner will get cold.
Dad	He's got to learn it's my house. And you shouldn't encourage him . . .

(*Fade*)

Waste ground near a river.

Martin	'Ello, Dave.
Dave	Wotcha.
Martin	Had your dinner?
Dave	No. Not hungry. They won't let me have a dog. At least me Dad won't.
Martin	Pity. I say, look at that bloke down by the bridge.
Dave	He's got a sack.
Martin	Look, he's putting that mongrel of his in it.

(*Barks*)

Dave	He's tying it up.
Martin	He's not going to throw it in the river, is he?
Dave	Let's get nearer.

(*Fade*)

Dave	He won't see us here.
Martin	He's putting bricks in.
Dave	He's throwing it in the river. Come on.
Martin	No. Wait till he's gone.
Dave	We can't let it drown.

(*Sounds of running*)

Dave	I'm going in. There it is.
Martin	It's deep.
Dave	Not much.

(*Splash of jumping in*)

Dave	Got it. Hold on. Take it, will you? It's heavy.
Martin	O. K. I think I've got it.
Dave	Open it up while I get out.
Martin	It's difficult, being wet.
Dave	Take my knife. Catch.

(*Sound of ripping*)

Martin	Done it. He's still alive.
Dave	Thank God. Poor little thing.

(*Fade*)

Dave's garden

Martin	Well, it's eaten a tin of dog meat. What shall we do with it?
Dave	I'm going to keep it.
Martin	What will your father say?

Dave	I shan't tell him. I'll find a way.
Martin	Good luck, mate. Are you dry yet?
Dave	Almost.

(*Fade*)

Dave	Fiona.
Fiona	What is it?
Dave	Here.
Fiona	Why?
Dave	I've got something.

(*Barks*)

Fiona	It's a dog.
Dave	It's mine. A chap threw it in the river and Martin and me rescued it.
Fiona	Dad won't let you keep it.
Dave	I'm not going to tell him.
Fiona	He's bound to find out. Where are you going to keep him?
Dave	In this shed, till I can think of what to do. He won't come in here again today, he's watching the telly.
Fiona	He'll find out.

Dave's house, early next morning.

(*Fade into snoring*)

Mum	Ernest! Ernest!
Dad	What?
Mum	Ernest! Wake up.
Dad	What is it?
Mum	I'm sure I can hear something.
Dad	You're always hearing something. Go back to sleep.
Mum	I can hear a noise downstairs.

Dad	What time is it?
Mum	Two o'clock.
Dad	I can't hear anything.
Mum	Listen. There it is again.

(*Barking*)

Mum	There's that dog barking.
Dad	So what?
Mum	The barking's coming from our garden. You must go and see what it is.
Dad	No.
Mum	Well, I'll go.
Dad	No you won't, I will. What a life! Disobedient children and now this.

(*Fade*)

Dave's Garden.

Policeman	O.K. What do you think you're doing?
Burglar	I've lost my way.
Policeman	Is this your house then, sir?
Burglar	I don't know. I'm lost.
Policeman	Somebody's left that window open. That's a bit stupid.
Burglar	So they have.
Policeman	All right. Just hand me that bag, will you?

(*Clanking sound*)

Policeman	Funny set of things to be carrying around at this time of night. Let's have a look at you. Well, well, it's Shifty Farmer.
Burglar	That damned dog!
Policeman	A law abiding citizen, I should call him.
Dad	W . . . What's going on?
Policeman	Are you the owner, sir?

Dad	Yes.
Policeman	This gentleman has just effected an entry into your premises. I think you'll find one or two of these things belong to you.
Dad	A burglar!
Policeman	One of the best. Shifty Farmer has honoured you with his presence.
Burglar	Shut up.
Dad	A dog woke us.
Policeman	Not yours?
Dad	We've not got a dog.
Dave	It was mine.
Dad	What are you doing up?
Dave	It was my dog.
Dad	What do you mean, yours?
Dave	My dog. I rescued it. I put it in the shed.
Dad	Did you?
Policeman	I'd like a statement from you, sir.

(*Fade*)

Dave's house.

Dave	There was Martin and me and we saw this bloke putting a dog in a sack and putting bricks in, too. Then he flung it in the river.
Mum	You didn't go in the river!
Dave	I did.
Mum	What a silly thing to do. No wonder your clothes were so dirty.
Dave	You couldn't let it drown.
Fiona	That's what I think.
Dad	I suppose you expect to keep it now?
Mum	Well, it did stop us getting burgled.
Fiona	Go on, Dad.
Dad	Well, I don't suppose the owner wants it back.

(*Barks*)

14

Dave	Look. He likes you.
Dad	O.K. You win. What are you going to call it?
Dave	Tiger, of course.

A Fairly Happy Ending

Characters:

Chris
Dave
Liz
Alan
Norma
Clive
Mandy
Mr Jones, a farmer
Morgan, his son

The action takes place on a mountain hillside.

Alan	It's stopped raining.
Norma	For how long?
Clive	Yes. And it's getting dark.
Mandy	How far is it to the hostel?
Dave	Five miles.
Liz	Five!
Dave	All of that.
Clive	Rotten old devil.
Mandy	We could at least have stopped in his barn.
Norma	It was his son frightened me most.
Liz	Half-witted by the look of him. Savage. They've

17

	lived alone up in these valleys so long that they're uncivilised.
Clive	He wasn't as savage as those dogs looked.
Alan	Yes. I was thinking of those. Hadn't we better be getting on? 'Get off my land. Get right off my land or I'll let these dogs loose,' he said. Aren't we still on his land?
Dave	We're far enough away. Besides, we could see 'em coming. The farm must be almost below us.
Norma	I think Alan's right. We should be moving. If those dogs come after us, I couldn't run to save my life.
Mandy	Nor me. And how shall we find the way, if it gets dark?
Clive	We'd best not wait too long.
Dave	Don't worry about finding the way. Chris knows this place like the back of his hand.
Alan	Famous last words.
Liz	He doesn't know it as well as you do, Dave.
Dave	Oh yes, he does. He's walked over these hills before. I can read a map all right. But that's not the same.
Alan	Fat lot of good a map is in the dark.
Liz	Can you read a map?
Alan	Never said I could. I'm an amateur like everyone else—except Dave. And Chris, of course.
Liz	What's Chris doing? Too high and mighty to be with the rest of us?
Dave	Chris?
Chris	Yes?
Dave	What's up?
Chris	Come here.
Clive	What are you looking at?

(*Follows* **Dave** *to where* **Chris** *is standing*)

Alan	Hang on. Let's have a look.
Liz	That's just like Chris. Ordering people about. I'm not walking a step further than I have to.
Norma	It might be interesting. You coming, Mandy?

18

Mandy	Might as well.
	(*She and* **Norma** *go over to the other group.* **Liz** *follows slowly*)
Chris	Down there. See?
Dave	No. I told you. It looks just like any other stream to me.
Alan	I can see it. I can see it now. See, Dave? That white rock.
Clive	And the earth underneath it. That other rock's holding it back. Spade-shaped.
Dave	Oh yes. I've got it now. That's recent. That fallen soil looks fresh.
Clive	And that big patch of grass. You can see where it's come from. Been torn out higher up.
Chris	Yes. And, if you look a bit higher still, there's a lot more ready to go.
Norma	Yes, but isn't that the water—the rain—bringing it down?
Mandy	You mean like the stream just broadening its bed? They do that, don't they?
Chris	That's not just the stream. I'd lay money there's water underground, too. Looks like the whole hillside could start to slip.
Liz	How dramatic can you get!
Chris	I'm not just being dramatic, Liz.
Dave	No, Liz. You take a good look. He could be right.
Liz	So what? It's probably happened before.
Chris	Maybe. But not like this. This stream serves the farm, if I'm right.
Liz	Good. They'll have muddy water to drink, then, won't they?
Dave	It's not as simple as that.
Chris	You see what I mean, Dave, eh?
Dave	It could be serious.
Chris	It could at that.
Alan	What are you two on about?
Chris	Perhaps you didn't notice. The farm backs on to a kind of cliff, the stream comes over that into a long pool and runs away round the farm.
Norma	Well?

Dave	If the hillside goes, it could shoot all this muck and these stones down on top of the farm.
Liz	Rubbish!
Chris	You can think what you like, Liz, but there's a chance.
Mandy	Serve him right.
Chris	Just for being a bad-tempered farmer? Someone could get hurt.
Clive	He'll know about it, won't he?
Chris	I don't reckon we should take that chance.
Liz	What do you suggest we should do, then? Get some stones and prop it all up?
Chris	No. We'll have to go down again and warn him.
Clive	You what?
Alan	If he sees you coming, he'll have those dogs snapping round your heels before you can get near enough to shout.
Norma	I'm not going.
Mandy	It'll take half an hour to scramble all that round-about way down.
Chris	No, it won't. I'll go.
Liz	No, you won't! Dave says that you're the only one that knows the way. I'm not hanging about up here in the pouring rain, waiting for you to come back.
Dave	Liz! I'll go, Chris. You can take the others on, and I'll catch up.
Liz	You go, Dave Barry, and I'll never speak to you again!
Alan	Why should anyone go? The farmer's lived up here all his life. He'll know about dangers like this.
Clive	Liz is right about the rain. It's beginning again.
Mandy	If we all wait here, we'll get soaked.
Norma	Look! There's something down there.
Chris	Where?
Norma	Under that rock on its end holding back the dirt. When it moved, I saw it.
Dave	You can just see its legs. Is it a sheep?
Chris	Too small. It's a lamb, isn't it?

Norma	Poor thing!
Liz	I can't see anything. It's a bit of stick.
Dave	There aren't any trees up here.
Liz	Well, what can we do about it?
Dave	Go down and pull it out?
Liz	And have all that earth fall on you? Don't be daft.
Norma	You can't just leave it there.
Mandy	If that earth comes down on top of it, it'll be buried alive.
Alan	It'll get out again.
Clive	And, if it doesn't, it's no great loss. It's due to be mutton anyway.
Mandy	Clive! Don't be so mean!
Chris	It's the farmer's loss. All the more reason for telling him.
Liz	I've told you. You can't leave us all up here on our own.
Dave	I'll settle this. It looks as though we're going to stand here arguing until it gets dark. Then we shall be in a spot. First, we'll free that lamb. Then Chris can go down to the farm and tell the farmer. I'll take the party on. There's some time before dark. I can map read us all over the next ridge. Chris can catch us up.
Liz	Dave! You're not going down there after that sheep. It's dangerous.
Dave	Oh, shut up, Liz. Right, Chris?
Chris	It saves the time it would take to get the farmer up here to rescue his own blooming lamb, but I don't know—
Norma	I can hear it bleating.
Alan	You can't hear anything over the noise of the water, you twit.
Dave	Right. I'll be back in a tick.

(*He begins to climb down into the gully*)

Liz	Dave! Be careful.
Chris	He's all right on this side of the stream. It's the other side that's slipping.

Liz	It's all very well for you to talk. You're safe up here aren't you?
Chris	Perhaps I should have gone.
Liz	It's a bit late now.
Alan	He's all right. He's waving.

(*Pause*)

Clive	He won't get down to it that way. He wants to try higher up.

(*Pause*)

Norma	What's he stopping for?
Liz	He's not stopping. He's picking his way. What do you expect him to do? Fly across the stream?

(*Pause*)

Mandy	He's there now. He's got it. It's all right. Look, it's running up the other bank.
Norma	Oh, it's sweet.
Alan	Sweet? It's a blooming nuisance, keeping us here. The knees of my trousers are sopping wet.
Chris	That's that, then. I'll get down to the farm. Dave'll take you on.
Clive	What's up with Dave? He's fallen.
Liz	I told you so. Don't just stand there. Go down and help him.
Alan	No. He's up again. He's all right.
Liz	He isn't! He's limping. He needs help.
Chris	You're right. Come on, Clive.

(**Clive** *and* **Alan** *follow* **Chris** *off to help* **Dave**)

Liz	I shouldn't be surprised if he's broken something. That's all we need.
Norma	He wouldn't be walking, if he'd broken something.
Mandy	They're giving him a hand. He doesn't look too bad.
Liz	All this would never have happened, if Chris hadn't started looking for landslides.
Mandy	He's all right, Liz, he's walking by himself.

Liz	He's not all right. He's limping.
Norma	This settles one thing.
Mandy	What?
Norma	Chris can't go down to the farm now. He'll have to stay with us and help Dave.
Mandy	You don't know Chris. He'll feel honour bound to help the farmer.
Liz	You don't know Dave. He'll want to let Chris go, if he can walk, and take us himself. They both want to be heroes.

(**Chris**, **Dave**, **Clive** *and* **Alan** *return.* **Dave** *is limping.*)

Liz	Dave! Are you all right?
Dave	Not so bad. I'll be slow but I can walk. I trapped my foot between two rocks and twisted it. The stones were shifting. Chris is right. That hillside's on the move. Chris will have to go down to the farm.
Liz	No, he won't. You're hurt.
Clive	You've got think of Dave first, Chris.
Dave	I told you—I'll manage. Chris?
Chris	Listen, you lot. I really should go. I mean—you've seen it now, close to. It is dangerous, isn't it?
Liz	Oh, don't start all that again.

(**Mr Jones** *and his son* **Morgan** *arrive*)

Mr Jones:	Off you go, you lot! I told you before—get off my land!
Chris	Now, wait a bit! We were going.
Mr Jones	Oh no you weren't. I was watching you from down the valley.
Alan	We were just having a rest at first. Besides—
Mr Jones	You weren't having a rest. I know your game. Hang about until dark. Then slip down and get into the barn. It's happened before. I know your sort. You're city people. You've no sense at all. Lighting matches. Breaking things.
Liz	No sense! It's you that's got no sense.

Mr Jones	I'm not standing here listening to your cheek. Get on your way. Morgan! Go and get the dogs out of the van.
Liz	You see, Chris! Thinking of helping people like that!
Chris	Just a minute, mister. We were waiting here because we were coming back to warn you.
Mr Jones	Warn me? About what? A likely tale.
Morgan	Give him a chance, Dad.
Chris	The hillside's due to come down. It could fall in your yard or even damage your house.
Morgan	I told you we should have kept an eye on it.
Mr Jones	Let's have a look. Morgan! He's right! We'd best get down to the village. Get some men to come up. We'll put up that boarding for protection like last time.
Liz	How about giving us all a lift down there, then? Dave sprained his ankle saving one of your sheep.
Mr Jones	There's no room.
Morgan	Oh, come on, Dad. We can take some of them.
Norma	Please. We're all wet through and tired.
Mr Jones	I dunno.
Chris	How about this? If your son runs the girls and Dave down to the village, me and Clive and Alan will come down with you and make a start on the work. Won't we?
Alan	I suppose so.
Clive	If there's nothing else for it.
Mr Jones	Right. Done. And we'd best get started. Morgan, you run the others down. Come on, then, lads. This way. You might even get some hot tea and supper out of it.
Clive	Cheerio, girls. See you later.
The girls	Cheers.

(**Mr Jones, Chris, Clive** and **Alan** *go off*)

Morgan	Shall we get moving, then? It's not far. I'm parked up a track the other side of that hill. Best part of a quarter of a mile.

Dave	Thanks a lot.
Morgan	It'll be a bit rough. I've got the dogs in the van and an ailing sheep.
Liz	That'll suit Norma. She thinks sheep are sweet.
Morgan	They smell a bit sheep do, you know. Specially when they're wet.
Mandy	I don't mind riding with a gorilla. Just as long as I'm sitting down and out of the wet.
Norma	Nor me.
Dave	Come on, then. Let's get walking and stop the talking.

The Mistake

Characters:

Miss Bennett
Mr Needham
The President
Mr Charles
Manager
Mrs Andrews
Mr Andrews
Gary
Tracy

The offices of the Cleanette Co. Ltd. **Miss Bennett** *enters.*

Miss Bennett	The President is on the phone, Mr Needham.
Mr Needham	The President! Needham here, sir.
The President	How are you, Needham?
Mr Needham	Very well, sir.
The President	Good. Just off for a round of golf myself. But before I go I would like to congratulate you.
Mr Needham	Congratulate me?
The President	Well, it was your idea in the first place.
Mr Needham	But I couldn't have done it without your backing.
The President	True, true. Anyway when I've toddled round eighteen holes I'll be over to tour the factory.
Mr Needham	About what time, sir?
The President	Oh—three I should think. Congratulations once again Needham.
Mr Needham	Miss Bennett!

Miss Bennett	Yes, Sir.
Mr Needham	The President is coming over here this afternoon to tour the factory. Alert everybody. I want the visit to go off like clockwork. Tidy up this office. Oh, Miss Bennett!
Miss Bennett	Yes, sir.
Mr Needham	He wishes to congratulate me on my ruse of disguising robots to look like washing machines. He told me last week that our internal security had been tip-top and nobody knows anything about it. Do you know what I think he's coming over for?
Miss Bennett	No, sir.
Mr Needham	We could win a large government contract.
Miss Bennett	I always told you it was a brilliant idea, sir. Especially as we make real washing machines as well.
Mr Needham	Yes, I can't tell the difference between the robots and the real washing machines myself. Never mind this office. I must prepare my speech of welcome first.
	(*He paces the room*)
	Mr President . . . no, honoured President . . . no, most honoured President . . . the workers and I . . . best to put the workers first to get in well with the union . . .
	(**Miss Bennett** *returns*)
Miss Bennett	Mr Charles wishes to see you, sir.
Mr Needham	Charles? Who's Charles?
Miss Bennett	A despatch clerk from 'C' shop, sir.
Mr Needham	A despatch clerk! I've no time to see despatch clerks. I'm preparing a speech for the President.
Miss Bennett	But he says it's urgent, sir.
Mr Needham	It will have to wait until the President has gone. Now how shall I put it? The workers and I are most gratified that you should visit us to see the fruits of our joint labour. This is a fine example . . .
Miss Bennett	He won't go away, sir.

Mr Charles	*(following her in)* Can I see you, sir?
Mr Needham	How dare you burst in here?
Mr Charles	It's urgent, sir.
Mr Needham	Get out!
Mr Charles	But a robot is missing, sir.
Mr Needham	A robot missing?
Mr Charles	I've counted twenty times, sir, and there's one short in Batch 23.
Mr Needham	Well, count again, man.
Mr Charles	But I think I sent it out with a batch of real washing machines, sir.
Mr Needham	You what!
Mr Charles	It was standing on the side, sir, for a minor repair by a fitter and I think my new assistant packaged it in a normal box which was despatched yesterday morning.
Mr Needham	Despatched!
Mr Charles	Yes, sir.
Mr Needham	Who were the retailers?
Mr Charles	Here, sir.
Mr Needham	Miss Bennett! Get me Ogden's. High Street, Wellingfield, immediately. Thank you. Cleanette Company here. The Managing Director speaking. I'm enquiring about a washing machine we despatched yesterday morning. No. T 2/23. We think there's a fault in it and naturally we are anxious to preserve our good name.
Manager	Just a minute, I'll check.
Mr Needham	He's checking.
Miss Bennett	I'm sure it'll be all right.
Mr Charles	It was the new assistant—see. I don't think he's got much . . .
Mr Needham	Why can't they hurry?
Manager	Did you say No. T 2/23?
Mr Needham	That's correct.
Manager	We've sold it.
Mr Needham	Sold it? But you couldn't have done.
Manager	That is my job, to sell things. Actually your machines are going like hot cakes.

Mr Needham	Well, can I please have particulars of the customer?
Manager	It was bought by a Mr Andrews of 14 Goss Way . . .

(*Fade*)

The home of Mr and Mrs Andrews

Mrs Andrews	Take it out of the box, Jim.
Mr Andrews	It's heavy. I'll have to cut out this side.
Gary	That's what it says on the box.
Mr Andrews	Thank you. I can read.

(*Sound of cutting*)

	There we are.
Mrs Andrews	Shall I try it out with this bit of washing?
Mr Andrews	No, leave it now, dear, and come and watch the telly.
Mrs Andrews	All right. Tracy, do the washing up, please.
Tracy	Oh, Mum! What about Gary?
Mrs Andrews	It's your turn.
Tracy	Rotten lot. I want to watch telly as well. Suffering cats! I wish I had something to do the washing up for me!

(*Whirring sound*)

	What's happening? The machine's lit up. It's moving. It's going to the sink. It's got arms. It's turning on the tap. Mum! Mum! Dad! come quick.
Mr Andrews	What's the matter?
Mrs Andrews	What is it, Tracy?
Tracy	Look!
Mrs Andrews	It's washing up.
Mr Andrews	Have they sent us a new-fangled dish washer? How did you start it, Tracy?
Tracy	I just said I wished I had something to do the washing up for me.
Gary	Look at the speed it works at.
Mrs Andrews	My dishes!
Tracy	It's finished.

30

Mr Andrews	You must have activated it in some way. Let's try it again. Get those tea cups from the front room, Gary.
Gary	Right.
Mr Andrews	Now you say the same words.
Mrs Andrews	Shouldn't we get on to the shop?
Tracy	I think I said, 'I wish I had something to do the washing up.'
Mr Andrews	It's not moving.
Gary	It hasn't lit up.
Tracy	Just a minute. What I actually said was, 'Suffering cats! I wish I had something to do the washing up for me!'

(*Whirring sound*)

Gary	It's working.
Mrs Andrews	Oh, dear.
Tracy	It's finished.
Mr Andrews	Do you know what I think? I think we've got our own robot. Let's see if it can do anything else. I'll have a go. Suffering cats! I wish I had something to hoover the front room for me.

(*Whirring sound*)

Tracy	It's moving around.
Mr Andrews	It's searching for the hoover. Put it in front of it, Gary, in here.
Gary	It's picking it up. Hooray.
Mr Andrews	Our own robot!
Tracy	The speed of it.
Mrs Andrews	Is it safe?
Mr Andrews	I wonder if it can cook.
Tracy	It's nearly finished.
Mr Andrews	Put some spuds and a pan on the table and see if it can cook some chips. You try it, Mum.
Mrs Andrews	I don't like to.
Gary	Go on.
Mrs Andrews	Very well. I wish I had—
Mr Andrews	No, you must start with 'Suffering cats!'

31

Mrs Andrews	I feel a fool.
Tracy	Go on, Mum.
Mrs Andrews	Suffering cats! I wish I had something to cook some chips.
Gary	It's going to the table.
Tracy	It's peeling the spuds.
Mr Andrews	We've got our own robot!
Mrs Andrews	No more peeling potatoes ever again!

(*Fade*)

Mr Andrews	Just think. When this programme is finished we'll have a meal waiting for us.
Mrs Andrews	I wonder what it's like with Chinese food.
Mr Andrews	Well, its breakfast was wonderful.

(*Doorbell rings*)

Mr Andrews	Someone at the door. I'll go. Make sure that door is locked, Mabel.

(*Voices heard*)

Mr Andrews	Well, come this way Mr Needham
Mr Needham	So, as I said, if we could have the machine back I'll give you another one without the fault.
Mr Andrews	I don't want it changed.
Mr Needham	But it's faulty.
Mrs Andrews	We want to keep it.
Mr Needham	I'll give you a de-luxe machine in its place.
Mr Andrews	No!
Mrs Andrews	No!
Mr Needham	Please!
Mr Andrews	We know why you want it back.
Mr Needham	You do?
Mr Andrews	Yes. It's a robot, isn't it?
Mr Needham	I can't comment. All I can say is that it's a dangerous thing to have around the house.
Mrs Andrews	We don't find it so. It's washed up. Hoovered the carpet. Cooked meals. It's even fed the dog.
Mr Andrews	Yes, and tomorrow we're going to see if it will decorate the house.

Mr Needham	I will have to report this to the President.

(Fade)

The offices of the Cleanette Co. Ltd. **Mr Needham** *is on the phone to the President.*

Mr Needham	Yes, sir.
The President	I want to take back everything I said about you.
Mr Needham	Yes, sir.
The President	You are an incompetent ass. You realise this could bring down the Government?
Mr Needham	Yes, sir.
The President	Whatever happens, you must get it back.
Mr Needham	Yes, sir.
The President	And keep it out of the papers.
Mr Needham	Yes, sir.
The President	I give you one week.

(Sound of phone being slammed down)

Mr Needham	Miss Bennett, what am I to do?
Miss Bennett	Try to appeal to his heart, sir.

(Fade)

The Andrews' house.

Mr Needham	I've come with this gentleman to make this final appeal to you, Mr Andrews.
Mr Charles	I'm a working man like you, Mr Andrews. I made the mistake about the robot. If we don't get it back, I'll get the sack and I've four children to keep.
Mr Andrews	I can't help that. That's your affair. This could be the big opportunity in my life. I could sell my story to the newspapers.
Mr Needham	Please don't do that. Can't you see what this means? It could put millions of people out of work, this robot: cooks, factory hands, domestics,

33

painters and decorators. The Government has had it made to work in top security areas. But should the unions get to hear of it, it will bring down the Government.

Mr Andrews	I'm not entirely made of steel, Mr Needham.
Mr Needham	You'll give it us back then?
Mr Andrews	No, I'll keep it but I'll say nothing to the news-papers and get my family to keep it a secret. I'll just have it working for me.

(*Fade*)

Cleanette Co. Ltd. offices.

Mr Needham	What shall I do, Miss Bennett? The week's nearly up. In thirty minutes I shall be fired. Have you any more ideas?
Miss Bennett	No, sir. (*Pause*) Mr Andrews, sir, to see you.
Mr Andrews	I'll come straight to the point. I want you to take that robot back.
Mr Needham	You do?
Mr Andrews	Yes it's ruining me. My wife has given up doing any housework. She's been out playing bingo all the week and it's costing me a fortune. She wants the house decorated again and it only did it six days ago. I just can't afford it. And my children will grow up ignorant and fat because it is cooking for them all the time and doing their homework.
Mr Needham	Say no more. We'll come straight away. Miss Bennett, get Mr Charles and a van.
Mr Andrews	You'll have to tackle my wife, Mr Needham. She won't want to let it go . . .

(*Fade*)

The Andrews' house.

Mrs Andrews	You're not going to have it back. This has liberated me. It has made me a free woman!
Mr Andrews	Be sensible dear.

34

Mrs Andrews	Just watch it do my knitting. Knit one plain, one purl. No, purl! You fool! Look at the pattern.
	(*Loud explosion*)
Mr Andrews	It's blown up!
Mr Needham	Thank goodness for that.
Mrs Andrews	What's gone wrong?
Mr Andrews	Are you all right, dear?
Mrs Andrews	My poor little Robbie.
Mr Needham	This pattern is the cause. Much too complicated for this mark of robot. It would throw it into confusion. Hence the explosion. I'm sorry for the damage but I'll send you a washing machine.
Mr Andrews	A de-luxe model.
Mr Needham	I'm afraid not, sir. Just the ordinary standard model you thought you had bought. And this time I will check it myself before it leaves the factory.

Grandmother's Clock

Characters:

Mr Rankin
Mrs Rankin
Peter ⎫ the Rankins' children
Lesley ⎭
Mrs Willis
Gran, Mr Rankin's mother
Mr Frobisher
Dennis, Mr Frobisher's assistant

The action takes place in the Rankins' sitting room.

Mrs Rankin	You'll *have* to talk to her. I don't just mean about getting rid of the sideboard. Though, I'd like to. Look at it. It is too big for a modern house.
Mr Rankin	The sideboard's a minor thing. Anyway she won't part with it. No, what bothers me is the change that's come over her. She was so different when she first came. So good with the children. Cheerful. I mean, they still like her. And you're very fond of her, aren't you?
Mrs Rankin	Strange? She's got shifty. So quiet. I don't like it.

(**Lesley** *comes in with* **Mrs Willis**)

Mrs Willis	I can't stop. My son's waiting outside. He gets so impatient.

37

Mrs Rankin	Oh? Gran will be down in a minute. She's getting ready to go out.
Mrs Willis	I would like to see her. We haven't met in weeks. But I must rush off.
Mrs Rankin	You haven't seen her for weeks? But she said—
Mrs Willis	She's dropped right out of sight. That's why I came. I thought I'd better let her have this book back.
Mr Rankin	Not seen her?
Mrs Willis	Not for weeks and weeks. Give her my love. Sorry I missed her. Thank her for the book. I must go.
Mrs Rankin	Of course. Shame you can't stop. Goodbye.

(**Mrs Willis** *goes out with* **Lesley**)

Peter	(*coming in*) What's up, Mum? You look worried.
Mrs Rankin	And Gran told us she was seeing Mrs Willis every week! You'll have to speak to her Joe.
Mr Rankin	I certainly will. We'll let her take the holiday money down town now and pay it into the account. But I'll have a long talk to her when she comes back.

(**Gran** *comes in, followed by* **Lesley**)

Mrs Rankin	Why, Gran! You're not ready to go out. We thought you were putting your things on.
Gran	I'm not going today.
Mr Rankin	Don't you feel well?
Gran	If you must know, I'm waiting for a man. He's calling this afternoon.
Peter	What man?
Gran	Just a man.
Mr Rankin	An old friend? Do we know him? Someone you've met?
Gran	He's coming on business.
Mr Rankin	Business?
Gran	I suppose you'll all have to know sooner or later. He's coming to buy the clock.
Mrs Rankin	Your clock?

38

Mr Rankin	Not that old clock! You can't.
Gran	Why not? It's mine.
Mr Rankin	But what do you want to sell it for? It belonged to your grandmother. It's an heirloom. It belongs to the family.
Gran	It belongs to me. And I want to sell it because I want some money.
Mr Rankin	For Heaven's sake, mother! You don't need money. You've got all you want here, haven't you?
Gran	I need some money.
Mrs Rankin	I was hoping that it would come down to us and then on to the children. You don't want to sell it, Gran. Not that lovely old clock.
Gran	Yes, I do.
Lesley	Let her do what she wants. It's her clock.
Mr Rankin	You're not going to sell that clock.
Peter	Why not? If she wants to.
Mrs Rankin	Gran! Be reasonable.
Gran	I am being reasonable. You don't know—
Mrs Rankin	Don't know what?
Gran	Never mind. Anyway, it's too late to argue. He'll be here any minute. I'll go and get it.
Peter	I'll fetch it for you, Gran.
Mr Rankin	Peter!
	(**Peter** *goes out of the room*)
Gran	Leave me alone, Joe. I must sell it. What else can I do?
Mrs Rankin	But you're so fond of it, Gran.
Gran	There are other things more important.
Lesley	Let her explain, Dad. She must have good reason.
Gran	I can't explain. Just let me be.
Lesley	There. You see. Now she's getting upset.
Mr Rankin	Not as upset as I am.
	(**Peter** *comes in with the clock*)
	Peter! I thought I told you! Take it back.
Peter	No.
Mr Rankin	Do as you're told. Here, give it me.

Peter	Leave it alone. It's hers.
Mr Rankin	Give it to me.

(*He grabs the clock. They are both clumsy. It falls to the floor.*)

Mrs Rankin	Joe! Look what you've done! It's broken.
Gran	Oh, don't say that. He won't buy it. Whatever shall I do?
Lesley	(*picking it up*) The glass is smashed and you cracked that lovely case.
Mr Rankin	Let me look. Good Heavens! Peter, this is all your fault.
Peter	Why me? You dragged it out of my hands.
Mr Rankin	And it's partly your fault, too, Gran. If you hadn't wanted to sell it, this would never have happened.
Mrs Rankin	Let me have a look. It might be repaired.
Gran	He won't want it now. Oh—I'm so ashamed.
Lesley	Ashamed? You didn't break it.
Peter	No, it was Dad, for all he says.
Mr Rankin	It was you, you young fool!
Mrs Rankin	Well, don't go on squabbling about it. It's done now.
Gran	You're right. The fat's right in the fire. How can I tell you?
Peter	Tell us what? Try. I'll bet I understand.
Gran	You'll never forgive me.
Lesley	Gran! Of course, we will.
Gran	I don't know where to start.
Mr Rankin	Calm down. Begin at the beginning.
Gran	That Mrs Burns! She's a wicked woman!

(*Pause. More gently*)

	No. I suppose she isn't. But I am.
Lesley	No, you're not, Gran.
Gran	I am. I am. I can't go on.
Mr Rankin	Yes, you can. What about Mrs Burns?
Gran	About two months ago, I met her one Saturday. I was weak and silly. She tempted me.

40

Peter	Tempted you?
Lesley	To do what?
Gran	I won the first time, you see.
Mr Rankin	Won? You don't mean—gambling?
Gran	Yes.
Mr Rankin	An occasional ten p on a horse? That's not so bad.
Gran	It wasn't ten p, Joe. It was pounds.
Mr Rankin	Pounds? Where did you get the money?
Mrs Rankin	The holiday money! Every week? All of it?
Gran	Yes.
Mr Rankin	On horses?
Gran	On Bingo. Mrs Burns took me in the first time and I won. So I went again. I've been there every Saturday since.
Mr Rankin	How much have you lost?
Gran	Most of it.
Peter	But that was our holiday money! Clothes and spending.
Lesley	Gran, how could you?
Mr Rankin	When you say most of it, how much do you mean?
Gran	About forty pounds.
Peter	But that was our money. It's almost like stealing.
Lesley	How selfish can you get?
Gran	I got frightened. I lost my head. I meant it all for the best.
Peter	A fine best.
Mrs Rankin	Peter!
Gran	You've all done so much for me, I wanted to do something in return. Mrs Burns said it was easy. I thought if I could increase the holiday money, it would be a nice surprise.
Peter	Some surprise!
Lesley	What a stupid way to go about it!
Mr Rankin	Be quiet, you two. You didn't stop when you began to lose?
Gran	When I lost I got scared. So I started doubling up.
Mr Rankin	But—even so—forty pounds!
Gran	I went on Wednesdays as well. I had more than one card.

41

Mrs Rankin	When you said you were going to the over-sixties club?
Gran	Yes. And I went some Thursday nights.
Mrs Rankin	Instead of the pictures?
Gran	Yes.
Lesley	But the holiday money! You must have been crazy.
Gran	I know. I was.
Mr Rankin	How much have we got for the holidays?
Gran	Seven pounds.
Peter	Seven! We'll never make that up. Not in the time.
Gran	That's why I wanted to sell the clock. I went to see this dealer, Mr Frobisher. He said, if it was as I described it, it could be worth money.

(*There is a ring at the bell*)

Mr Rankin	That'll be him.
Gran	And he's come all the way across town, too.
Peter	I'll tell him to go away.
Mr Rankin	No, we'd better have him in, if only to explain.
Mrs Rankin	I'll let him in.

(*She goes out*)

Lesley	I suppose this means that we may not go on holiday at all.
Mr Rankin	We'll have to see.
Gran	I'm sorry.
Lesley	Sorry!

(**Mrs Rankin** *brings in* **Mr Frobisher** *and* **Dennis** *his assistant*)

Mrs Rankin	This is Mr Frobisher, everyone.
Mr Rankin	I'm sorry, Mr Frobisher. I'm afraid you've come for nothing. The fact is, we've had a bit of an accident with the clock.
Mr Frobisher	What a marvellous sideboard! What?
Mrs Rankin	The clock. It's broken.
Mr Frobisher	Broken? Take a look at it, Dennis.

42

Peter	Dad dropped it.
Mr Rankin	That'll do, Peter.
Dennis	Cost the best part of a fiver to get this right again.
Mr Frobisher	Let me look. No, it's not what I expected, anyway.
Mr Rankin	That's it then. I didn't think you'd want it.
Mr Frobisher	You see, besides being a dealer, I do some interior decorating. I have a rather rich customer who's interested in these things. I though he would have been interested, if the clock had been right.
Mr Rankin	Yes—well—nothing more to be said, is there?
Mr Frobisher	Oh, I think there is. What would you take for that sideboard?
Mr Rankin	We hadn't thought about it.
Gran	The sideboard?
Mrs Rankin	Mother's had it a long time. She's very attached to it.
Gran	How much would you offer?
Dennis	Let me have a look at it.
Mrs Rankin	Gran, are you sure you know what you're doing?
Mr Rankin	Don't do anything too suddenly. We can probably borrow money for the holidays.
Gran	I know what I'm doing, Joe. It's been well looked after, Mr Frobisher.
Dennis	There's no worm in it. Most of the carving is still there.
Gran	All of the carving is still there.
Mr Frobisher	A bit worn.
Gran	Not much. It's not really marked.
Dennis	You might do worse, Mr Frobisher. Say forty pounds.
Gran	Sixty.
Mr Frobisher	I wouldn't go more than fifty.
Gran	Make it fifty-five.
Mr Frobisher	I'll tell you what I'll do. I'll give you fifty and have your clock repaired. I've got a good man who can do it. You'll never know it's been damaged. it would cost you a lot more than a fiver to get it done.
Gran	All right.

Mr Frobisher	Good. I can give you a cheque now. I'll send the men round for it on Monday, if that's convenient, Mrs Rankin.

(*He writes the cheque*)

Mrs Rankin	Oh—I suppose so. But—Gran—are you sure?
Gran	I'm sure. I never liked it. It's you two I'm sorry for.
Mrs Rankin	What?
Gran	Jim's mother gave it us when we were married. He liked it. I didn't have the heart to say anything while he was alive. When I came here I brought it because you and Joe seemed so fond of it.
Mrs Rankin	We? Fond of it? Oh, I know we said—. Never mind. All's well that ends well.
Mr Frobisher	Thank you, Mrs Rankin.

(*Gives the cheque to* **Gran**)

	I have to get back now. Excuse me for rushing off.
Gran	Thank you Mr Frobisher.
Mr Frobisher	Dennis, carry the clock to the car, would you? Don't worry. We'll see ourselves out.
Mrs Rankin	It's no trouble. Peter—go and open the front door for Mr Frobisher's assistant.
Gran	Thank you, again, Mr Frobisher. Goodbye.
Mr Frobisher	On the contrary, Mrs Rankin—thank you. Goodbye everyone.

(**Peter** *goes out first, followed by* **Dennis, Mrs Rankin** *and* **Mr Frobisher**)

Lesley	I'm sorry for you about that sideboard, Gran.
Gran	I'm not. You don't think I could draw out five pounds of this, Joe? It might be my lucky afternoon.
Mr Rankin	No I'll come down with you and we'll pay it in together.
Gran	Not—perhaps—just one pound? It's been a lucky afternoon so far. I feel lucky.

Mr Rankin	Mother—I said, 'No!'.
Gran	Maybe you're right. We'll pay it all in. I'll go and get my coat. It seems a pity, though.

(*She goes out.* **Mr Rankin** *stands looking after her, shaking his head and clicking his tongue.*)

Lesley	I'll make us all a cup of tea, Dad. We need it.

Ghost Train

Characters:

Brian
Bob
Mum
Conductor
Pat
Glynis
A Fortune Teller
Chris
Lady Stall-holder

School.   (*Playground sounds*)

Brian	Are you going to the fair tonight?
Bob	Yeh, I've been saving up for weeks.
Brian	They reckon they've got more rides this year.
Bob	Yeh. I wanted to see them being put up but I had to go out for my Mum. She's a right drag lately.
Brian	What time shall we go? Seven?
Bob	No, it's more fun when it's darker. What about the 8.30 bus?
Brian	Sure. See you there.

(*Bell*)

Bob	I'd better go. We've got Percy next. He kicks up hell, if you're late.
Brian	See you then.

(*Fade*)

Bob's house.

Bob	But, Mum—!
Mum	I don't ask you to do much. I slave for you most of the year, my boy.
Bob	But, Mum—!
Mum	Anyone would think you were ashamed to take your sister.
Bob	But I've arranged to go with Brian!
Mum	He's got a sister as well.
Bob	But he won't be with her.
Mum	You know what happened to your sister last year. I just don't want her going on her own.
Bob	But she's such a drag.
Mum	How can you say that? I don't know what's got into you lately. If only your father was here, he wouldn't let you treat me like this.
Bob	All right I'll take her. But she'll have to come home when I want to.
Mum	Only she looks forward to it so much. You could go again tomorrow night on your own.
Bob	Yeh, I suppose I could do that.

(*Fade*)

Bus-stop.

Bob	I had to bring her.
Glynis	Charming! Don't think I wanted to come with you. It's just Mum. She exaggerates what happened last year.
Brian	My sister's coming as well.
Glynis	Where is she?
Brian	Round the corner. Her shoe came off.
Glynis	Pat! Pat!
Bob	That's mucked up the evening right proper.
Brian	Well, they'll just have to do what we want.
Bob	I'm going tomorrow night to do it properly.
Brian	Yeh, I'll save some money too. Here's the bus. Come on Pat.

48

On the bus.	*(Sound of bus)*
Conductor	Upstairs only. Hurry on. Get your fares ready, please.
Pat	We needn't sit with them.
Glynis	I didn't want to come with him.
Pat	No more did I want to come with our Brian.
Glynis	She doesn't like me out of her sight since last year. It was only that drunken man.
Pat	When my Mum heard about you she said I couldn't go to the fair on my own again. Oh look at that lady!
Glynis	The bus is going to hit her.
	(Screech of brakes)
Pat	Are you all right?
Glynis	Just bumped my head a bit.
Pat	Look, she's lying on the ground.
Glynis	I hope she's all right.
	(Fade)
Bob	Well, that's an hour we've been sitting here.
Brian	Goodness knows what time we'll get to the fair.
Bob	It'll be shutting.
Brian	No, it goes on late.
Bob	I only hope there's a bus back.
Brian	Yeh, there's special late buses.
Glynis	Is she all right?
Conductor	Broke her leg I think. She was also shaken up a lot.
Bob	When are we going? We've got to get to the fair.
Conductor	So have a lot of others, mate. The Policeman's still taking statements downstairs.
Bob	What a night!
	(Fade)
Fairground.	*(Noises of screams and fairground music)*
Bob	Here we are at last.

Brian	It's great. A lot of people are going home though.
Bob	Yeh, I like it best when it's packed.
Pat	We're going to the fortune teller first.
Brian	Oh no, not that rubbish.
Pat	Yes, the girls at school say she was ever so good last year and we never went.
Glynis	A lot of what she said came true.
Bob	It's all a big trick. Waste of money.
Glynis	Well, I'm going and I'll tell our Mum if you don't come with me.
Bob	Well, if we do we'll pick the next ride.
Brian	The Jets.
Bob	Yeh, the Jets.

(*Fade*)

Another part of the fair.

Brian	That's another quarter of an hour wasted. I don't think there is a fortune teller.
Glynis	There must be.
Bob	We've got to the end of the fair. There's no more. There aren't any people down here.
Pat	Let's just go round the corner. Look! There's her caravan down there next to the ghost train.
Glynis	Come on.
Bob	We're not wasting our money.
Glynis	We'll go by ourselves but you must wait.

(*Fade*)

The Fortune Teller's caravan.

| Fortune Teller | You are a very pretty girl and I see a very interesting future for you. Show me your hand. Yes, it's all written here, duck. You will have a long life but with several ups and downs. But you will come through them all right. You will, however, have to endure an illness which will worry your friends. Now I see, yes, I see a dark man. But he |

50

does not stay in your life for long. Now, I see a fair man. Yes, and I see children one, two, three. And I see money, quite a lot of money from an unexpected source. And I see the sea and a long journey for you. I can see no more, duck. May good luck always be with you. Girls! Come back here a minute! I want to warn you that shortly you could endure a very terrifying experience. But you must bear it. All will come well. All will come well. All will come well. Ah, the flames . . . the flames . . . the flames. My poor Bobby all on fire.

(*Fade*)

Glynis	Oh, she did scare me at the end.
Pat	What did she mean 'the flames'?
Glynis	And her face looked different as we came out.
Pat	Yes, it was as though you could see a skull through her skin.
Glynis	She didn't take any money either.
Pat	Perhaps it's all a trick. I wonder who the fair man will be. And she knew I wanted to emigrate to Australia, telling me about the long sea journey.
Bob	Come on. You've been hours.
Brian	It's our turn now and we want to go on this ghost train. We think it's a good one.
Glynis	I don't know if I dare.
Pat	That fortune teller scared us.
Bob	Well, you wanted to go.
Pat	No, she was ever so good really. Doesn't this ghost train look old-fashioned?
Brian	Yes, I reckon it's one of those good old-fashioned ones Dad is always telling us about.

(*Screams*)

Listen to the screams. Come on.

Bob	I say, he didn't take my money.
Brian	No, he just waved me in. He looked a bit queer to me.

Bob	Yeh, his bones seemed to stick out. His fingers were so thin. Here we go.
Brian	It's dark.
Bob	It's cold too.
Brian	Yes, I'm freezing.
Bob	Nothing's happening. What an evening! It's a swizz.
Brian	I reckon so. Still we got in free.
Bob	It's getting colder.
Brian	Look! A skeleton!
Bob	And another.
Brian	There's two more over there!
Bob	Look, a kind of white smoke.
Brian	I can't see. Coo, this is good.

(*Screams*)

Bob	Listen to those screams. There are those skeletons again in the mist. That's clever, they're running about. I wonder how they do that.
Brian	This is the best ghost train I've been in.

(*Girls' screams*)

	Listen to the girls behind.
Glynis	Bob! I'm frightened. Where are you?
Bob	Isn't it just great?
Brian	We're falling over!
Bob	We've crashed.
Brian	We'd better get out.

(*Screams from the girls*)

Pat	Brian, where are you? We've fallen out.
Brian	Over here.
Bob	Look! It's like green flames flickering.
Glynis	Get me out.
Brian	I think the roof's falling in.
Bob	Look, that skeleton's showing the way out.

(*Screams*)

Bob	There's the door. Come on.

52

(Fade)

Outside the Ghost Train.

Glynis	Thank God we're out of that.
Brian	It's all right. It was all part of the show. Everything's still here. We must tell them at school about this. Best ghost train ride I've ever had. I wonder how they do it?
Pat	I never want to go on anything like that again.
Bob	Let's go on the Jets.

   (Fade)

The playground.

Brian	I tell you it was great.
Chris	And I tell you you're a liar. There's no ghost train at the fair.
Bob	Well, we went on it.
Chris	Me and John went on everything and there was no ghost train.
Bob	I bet you.
Chris	Twenty p.
Bob	Right, you're on. We'll show you tonight.

   (Fade)

The Fairground.

Bob	Come on, it's down here. Round this next corner.
Chris	There's nothing round there.
Bob	Just you see. It's gone!
Chris	There you are, just an empty field. Twenty p please.
Bob	It was here last night.
Brian	We both went on the ghost train. There was a fortune teller's caravan over there as well.
Chris	Twenty p.

Brian	It must have moved. I'll ask that lady on the coconut stall. Hey, what's happened to the ghost train?
Lady	There's no ghost train.
Brian	What about the fortune teller?
Lady	There's no fortune teller either.
Chris	Twenty p, please.

(*Fade*)

School.

Glynis	Bob, Bob. Look what we've found in the history room.
Bob	What is it?
Pat	It's a cutting from an old local paper.
Glynis	Look it's dated 1923. Read it.
Bob	'Tragedy at the Fair. Last night a fortune teller's caravan and a ghost train were burnt down. The fortune teller and her cat were killed and six people, including the owner, were killed in the ghost train. The owner lost his life helping to rescue people.'
Pat	I feel all peculiar.
Brian	I knew there was something odd about it.
Bob	Nobody will believe us, but perhaps we are the only people in the world to have been on a ghost ghost train.

Foiled Again

(An old-fashioned melodrama)

Characters:

Sir Jasper Devenish
Uriah Creepe
Widow Frailbody
Lavinia Frailbody
Hector Sturdily
Nelly Whortleberry
Moses Ploddington
Enoch Strine

Narrator

*The **Narrator** is necessary only for a tape-recording. In a live performance, what he says may be used as stage directions.*

Narrator	The scene is the home of the Widow Frailbody and her daughter, Lavinia. Lavinia, the beautiful heroine, is saying farewell to the handsome hero, Hector Sturdily.
Hector	Duty calls, my dear. I must away.
Lavinia	Alas, dear Hector! Is there no help for it? What of marriage! My mother would not say nay.
Hector	It is not your mother I want to marry. And I would not have *you* marry a pauper. The dastardly Sir Jasper has seized my little farm in payment for a debt I owed him. Now I am penniless, I will

55

	go and seek my fortune elsewhere. I will serve my queen and country.
Lavinia	Ah, Hector, you are too brave. War is so dangerous. Can you not win wealth another way?
Hector	Not now, my dear. I have signed my name. I cannot leave the army unless I buy my way out. But it is my hope that I shall win glory and riches in battle. And then—
Lavinia	Then?
Hector	No longer a shameful pauper, I shall return and ask for your hand.
Lavinia	That you shall have, my love. My heart is yours already.
Hector	Ah, may that day soon come!
Narrator	Nelly Whortleberry, the Frailbodys' maid, comes in.
Nelly	Master Sturdily, there is a sergeant and two soldiers outside. They have come for you.
Hector	Oh, woe! My fatal hour has come. I can no longer stay.
Lavinia	This parting kills me.
Hector	Oh, Lavinia! Lavvy! Lav! My love! Farewell!
Narrator	He goes out with his arm across his eyes.
Lavinia	Hector! Oh, grief!
Narrator	She swoons.
Nelly	Miss Lavinia!
Narrator	While Nelly bends over Lavinia, Widow Frailbody enters and stands thunderstruck.
Widow	My daughter!
Nelly	Fainted, ma'am. She will recover. She could not bear to be sundered from Master Sturdily.
Widow	This is all the work of the dastardly Sir Jasper. He has taken Hector's land and now seeks to have mine. He came but lately to ask me to be his wife. But I saw through his plan. I spurned him and yet I fear him still. He is an evil villain.
Nelly	A wicked schemer.
Widow	His proposal brought back tragic memories. Years ago, Enoch Strine, the uncle of young Hector

	would have married me. Sir Jasper drove him out, too. Many times have I wondered what has become of Enoch.
Nelly	Perhaps he will return one day.
Widow	I pray for it. He would be my protector in this wicked world. I have great need of protection.
Nelly	You are not alone, ma'am. You have me and the aid of my betrothed, Moses Ploddington, the village constable.
Widow	Thank you, Nelly. You calm my fears. Come, Nelly, let us take Lavinia to her room. She may recover in quiet.
Narrator	The next scene takes place in the ancestral home of Sir Jasper Devenish, the evil local squire.
Sir Jasper	Uriah! Where is the fellow? Without him my plan may fail. Uriah!
Uriah	At your service, Sir Jasper.
Sir Jasper	Where have you been?
Uriah	This morning, as you bid me, I insured the life of the Oldest Inhabitant of the village. I have just been sawing through the bridge across which he makes his way home from the 'Dog and Duck' every night.
Sir Jasper	Splendid, my good fellow. You have done well. The insurance comes to me, does it?
Uriah	Almost immediately, sir, I should think.
Sir Jasper	Good, good. Now I have other work for you. I want Widow Frailbody's land—and her daughter, if I can.
Uriah	You seek to own the rich coalfield that lies under her land and the land of Hector Sturdily?
Sir Jasper	I do. Hector Sturdily's land I hold. I will own it outright when the mortgage payment falls due at the end of the month. He cannot pay me. The Widow Frailbody has refused my offer of marriage. I will go after the daughter.
Uriah	But marrying the daughter will not get you the land, master.
Sir Jasper	She will inherit it. I, as her husband, will own it.

57

Uriah	Inherit it? But her mother still lives.
Sir Jasper	Her mother may have an accident quite soon.
Uriah	I get your drift, master. How?
Sir Jasper	Go and visit the Widow and pay her my respects. Say I hope she bears me no malice. Say I bear her none for refusing my offer of marriage. Invite her perhaps to taste of this delicious cordial from this flask.
Uriah	But that is your flask, master.
Sir Jasper	No, no, Uriah, I have my own here.
Narrator	He shows Uriah the other hip flask.
Sir Jasper	The one you have is filled with a subtle Asiatic poison that kills without trace. When she has drunk from it, it will look like heart failure.
Uriah	Fiendishly cunning, master. But—a thought strikes me! What if she doesn't like cordial?
Sir Jasper	Pour it in her tea, when she isn't looking.
Uriah	Ha! Clever! But—ah—what if there is no tea?
Sir Jasper	Here is a bunch of flowers. Offer them to her. Invite her to savour their delicious odour. They are sprinkled with the same poisonous dust. That will be the last of her.
Uriah	And, if she has hay fever? If she doesn't care for flowers?
Sir Jasper	Gad, stap me and zounds! Hit her with a chair and feign an accident! Don't bother me with the details. Get rid of her!
Uriah	At once, master.
Sir Jasper	Wait! I have not finished yet. Here is a letter. I will read it to you. 'My darling Lavinia, come to the level-crossing at the hour of eight tonight. I shall be eagerly waiting. I have news. Yours eternally, Hector Sturdily.' Little will she know that I have penned this and forged Hector's hand. Hand it to Miss Lavinia secretly. Go. You will be well rewarded.
Uriah	Your wish is my command, master.
Narrator	With the next scene we are back at Widow Frailbody's. Uriah is ushered in to see the Widow by Nelly.

Uriah	Greetings, good lady. Sir Jasper has sent me to pay you his regards. He fears his offer of marriage may have offended you.
Widow	Not at all.
Narrator	She speaks softly to herself.
Widow	Little does Uriah know that I am hiding my true feelings. I tremble at the mention of Sir Jasper's name.
Narrator	She speaks to Uriah.
Widow	Pray, let me offer you some refreshment, Mr Creepe.
Uriah	Let me offer you some. Taste of this delicious cordial.
Narrator	He shows her the flask. The Widow shakes her head.
Widow	What a pretty flask! But—no, thank you. Strong drink has never yet passed my lips. Let us take a cup of tea together. Nelly!
Nelly	Yes, ma'am?
Widow	Please bring us tea. And who is that you have with you in the kitchen?
Nelly	It is Moses Ploddington, the village constable, ma'am. He has paused a while to rest his feet.
Widow	Very well, Nelly. Bring the tea.
Narrator	Nelly makes a curtsey and goes out.
Widow	And how is Sir Jasper, Mr Creepe?
Uriah	Thriving, ma'am, thriving, thank you kindly.
Narrator	He speaks softly to himself.
Uriah	Little does she know that she is playing into my hands. Sir Jasper is likely to thrive even better after the tea is brought.
Narrator	Nelly re-enters.
Nelly	Here is the tea, ma'am. I had the pot warmed and the water boiling.
Widow	Thank you, Nelly. You may go. Sugar, Mr Creepe?
Uriah	No, thank you ma'am. I fancy I am sweet enough.
Widow	Teehee, Mr Creepe. You are a droll. There is your cup.
Uriah	Thank you. Bless my soul! What a funny bird!
Widow	Where?

Uriah	Outside the window. Look!
Narrator	She does so and he pours from the flask into her cup.
Widow	I can't see anything.
Uriah	No, ma'am. It flew away.
Widow	Is the tea to your liking, Mr Creepe?
Narrator	They are both drinking tea. Uriah is studying the Widow closely.
Uriah	Very much so, ma'am.
Widow	A nice day, Mr Creepe.
Uriah	It is. And a nice room you have here. Some nice solid chairs. Is the tea to your liking, ma'am?
Widow	It is, thank you.
Uriah	Not too hot? Tastes all right?
Widow	It is most refreshing, thank you Mr Creepe.
Narrator	Nelly enters somewhat flustered.
Nelly	Oh, ma'am come quickly. I fear there is dirty work afoot.
Widow	Gracious! Excuse me, Mr Creepe.
Narrator	She hurries out after Nelly.
Uriah	Certainly, Mrs Frailbody. A fortunate interruption. Hm. Why has the Widow not succumbed to the tea? I will taste her cup and see. Hm. Tastes good, smells good. No ill-effects. Can Sir Jasper's plan have miscarried? Perhaps the flowers are harmless, too?
Narrator	He sniffs at them.
Uriah	Aargh! My hour has come! Oorgh!
Narrator	He staggers about the room and finally falls across the sofa. The Widow returns.
Widow	Lavinia! She is nowhere in the house. My mind misgives. Oh, Mr Creepe! Whatever is the matter?
Narrator	She goes across to him and looks more closely.
Widow	Eek! Help, oh, help!
Narrator	Nelly rushes in with Constable Ploddington.
Moses	Evening, Mrs Frailbody. Evening, Mr Creepe. Not feeling too well?
Widow	Mercy on us, Constable! He seems to be dead.
Moses	Very suspicious. No one must leave the house.

60

Widow	But we must out and seek my daughter. She has disappeared.
Nelly	This note may explain, ma'am. It asks Miss Lavinia to be at the level-crossing at eight. Look.
Widow	Heavens! It is signed, 'Hector'.
Uriah	I must confess before my last breath is drawn. Sir Jasper wrote the note. Ah!
Narrator	He falls back, really dead this time.
Moses	The plot thickens. We must to the level-crossing at once.
Narrator	They all rush out. The scene changes to the level-crossing. It is dark.
Lavinia	Hector! Oh, Hector, my love!
Sir Jasper	Ha! At last I have you in my power.
Lavinia	Sir Jasper! What does this mean?
Sir Jasper	It is my hour of triumph. It means you must yield to me.
Lavinia	Never. Never. I would rather die than say yes.
Sir Jasper	Then die you shall. If you refuse to marry me, I'll tie you to the railway line. The eight-fifteen is almost due.
Lavinia	Alas, I am undone. But I will not marry you. Death before dishonour.
Sir Jasper	You have once chance left.
Lavinia	Once chance? I'll take it, if it is honourable.
Sir Jasper	Sign this paper.
Lavinia	What is it?
Sir Jasper	No questions. Sign it, curse you. Or would you rather have the railway line? Would you rather marry me?
Lavinia	I will sign it.
Narrator	She does so.
Sir Jasper	Success! It is your will. You have left everything to me. Now, marry me or not the land is mine. Will you be my bride?
Lavinia	Never. And the will is worthless. The land is still my mother's.
Sir Jasper	Foolish girl. I think of everything. The land is

	already yours by inheritance. Your mother is no more. Uriah Creepe has done for her.
Lavinia	Oh, direst cruelty! I am quite lost!
Narrator	She faints.
Sir Jasper	A lucky stroke. Like this I can carry her to the railway line without a struggle. Ha! What is this? Who comes?
Narrator	Out of the darkness step Hector and Enoch Strine.
Hector	Unhand that lady, Sir Jasper!
Sir Jasper	Curses! I am foiled. Hector Sturdily! How did you come here? And who is with you?
Enoch	The bridge across the river is down. Our detour brought us this way, unfortunately for you, you villain. I, sir, am Enoch Strine.
Sir Jasper	Enoch Strine! My former enemy?
Enoch	Your enemy still, Sir Jasper. Little did you think, when you drove me out that I would return to spoil your hour of triumph. Here, take this bag of gold. Your dastardly schemes have come to naught.
Sir Jasper	Ha! What do you mean?
Enoch	I know about the coalfield. This bag of gold will pay the debt on the farm of my nephew, Hector. What have you to say to that?
Sir Jasper	Say to that? I have a deal to say to that. The law will be on my side.
Narrator	The Widow, Nelly and Moses Ploddington rush on.
Widow	There you are wrong, Sir Jasper. The law will give you your just deserts.
Sir Jasper	Thunder and lightning! The Widow Frailbody, curse her! How did she come here? Uriah should have rendered her lifeless.
Nelly	I heard that. Now I see it all. You plotted to murder my mistress but your plans have recoiled on your own head. And you would have dealt wickedly with Miss Lavinia, too.
Widow	Heaven protect her! I hope she has come to no harm.
Hector	Lavinia, Lavinia! My love! Speak to me.

62

Lavinia	Hector? Is it you? Where am I?
Hector	You are safe, my dear, in spite of all his evil plots.
Nelly	Moses! Do your duty. Arrest that villain. He has caused the death of his creature, Creepe, and he would have been the death of Miss Lavinia.
Moses	Ah! Sir Jasper, I have to warn you that anything you say may be taken down and used in evidence. I arrest you for murder and attempted kidnapping.
Sir Jasper	Lies! All lies!
Moses	There is also a little matter of the Oldest Inhabitant. He has brought a complaint against you. He says you caused him to fall in the river. We met him coming along. What have you to say to that?
Sir Jasper	More lies. A plot against me.
Narrator	He speaks softly to himself.
Sir Jasper	Things are happening too fast. My brain reels. A drink from my flask will refresh my scattered wits.
Hector	You cannot deny it, Sir Jasper. Your doom is sealed.
Sir Jasper	Deny it? I scorn your feeble accusations.
Narrator	He drinks.
Sir Jasper	Glug! Argh! What is this? I am poisoned. I have taken the wrong flask. Uriah took mine, the harmless one, and I am left with the venom. Alas, my hour has struck! Curses!
Narrator	He dies in great agony.
Enoch	So perish all such wicked men.
Widow	I know that voice. Enoch! You have returned to me.
Enoch	I have returned a wealthy man. Will you marry me?
Widow	Do I hear aright? It has been my wish this many a long year. Oh, Enoch!
Hector	Lavinia, my love. Nothing now stands in the way of our marriage. Is your mind still the same?
Lavinia	My mind and my heart are yours, my dear, and shall be as long as life shall last.

63

Hector	Lavinia, my love!
Nelly	Moses, you will receive promotion for this night's work. Have you nothing to say to me?
Moses	Nelly, I have. Will you consent to be my bride?
Nelly	Oh, Moses!
Widow	But what of Sir Jasper—and his creature, Uriah Creepe?
Enoch	Of the next world, I know nothing. But in this world, they have only one last help. Let us go and seek them out.
Widow	You mean?
Enoch	The vicar and the gravedigger. Come, let us go.